Miss Bindergarten Takes a with Kindergarten

by **JOSEPH SLATE**
illustrated by **ASHLEY WOLFF**

PEARSON

Glenview, Illinois • Boston, Massachusetts • Chandler, Arizona •
Upper Saddle River, New Jersey

Text copyright © 2001 by Joseph Slate
Illustrations copyright © 2001 by Ashley Wolff
All rights reserved.

This version of Miss Bindergarten Takes a Field Trip
published by Pearson.

ISBN 13: 978-0-328-47233-8
ISBN 10:   0-328-47233-6

2 3 4 5 6 7 8 9 10 V008 13 12 11 10

Today is field trip day. . . .

Adam's dad's a chaperone.

Brenda's mom is, too.

Christopher says,
"Hey, don't leave yet—
a stone hopped
in my shoe."

5

6

Miss Bindergarten goes to the

bakery with kindergarten.

Danny cuts
some cookies out.

Emily sees
them bake.

Franny squirts pink icing on a scrumptious chocolate cake.

Now Miss Bindergarten goes to the

fire station with kindergarten.

Gwen McGunny
rings a bell.

Henry holds
a hose.

12

Ian makes a funny face
and laughs as his nose grooows.

Jessie learns
Stop, Drop, and Roll.

Kiki tries
on gear.

Miss Bindergarten slides down the pole, and *L*enny gives a cheer.

Now Miss Bindergarten goes to the

post office with kindergarten.

17

Matty picks
the planet stamps.

Noah taps
The locks.

Ophelia asks where letters go when you slide them through the slots.

Patricia steers
    a canvas cart.

Quentin checks
    the scale.

Now Miss Bindergarten goes to the

library with kindergarten.

Sara grabs her favorite chair.

Tommy hugs a book.

Mr. Mack clicks the mouse.
"Here, Ursula, take a look!"

Vicky likes hot-air balloons.

Wanda loves the ships.

26

"A book is like a ticket to all sorts of splendid trips."

Now Miss Bindergarten goes to the

park with kindergarten.

Xavier shouts, "Where's Brenda's mom?"

Yolanda looks behind her.

"Don't worry. She's not lost,"
says Zach.

"I know where we can find her."

Now Miss Bindergarten goes—whoa!

stops!—with kindergarten.

33

Adam's dad sets out the cups.

Brenda's mom pours punch.

Miss Bindergarten cuts the cake . . .

. . . and they all sit down

to munch!

Did you see these shapes?

we saw these shapes

at the bakery

we saw these shapes

at the
fire station

circle

square

triangle

rectangle

diamond

38

we saw these shapes

we saw these shapes

we saw these shapes

at the post office

at the library

in the park

FRAGILE

hexagon

star

oval

heart

39